W9-ASP-165
3 4050 0000 6520 6

A ROOKIE READER

DIRTY LARRY

By Bobbie Hamsa

Illustrations by Paul Sharp

Prepared under the direction of Robert Hillerich, Ph.D.

CHILDREN'S PRESS
A Division of Grolier Publishing
Sherman Turnpike
Danbury, Connecticut 06816

Library of Congress Cataloging in Publication Data

Hamsa, Bobbie.
Dirty Larry.

(A Rookie reader)
Includes index.
Summary: Dirty Larry is never clean except when he is in the shower.
[1. Cleanliness — Fiction] I. Sharp, Paul, ill.
II. Title. III. Series.
PZ7.H1887Di 1983 [E] 83-10079
ISBN 0-516-02040-4

Printed in the United States of America.

18 19 R 02 01 00 99 98

Dirty Larry gets dirty.

No matter where he goes.

Dirty fingers.
Dirty hands.

Dirty face.

Dirty clothes.

Dirty feet.

Dirty seat.

Dirty knees.

Dirty nose.

Dirty eyes.

BY LARRY

FINGER PAINT

Dirty ears.

Dirty neck.

Dirty toes.

Dirty Larry gets dirty.
No matter what the hour.

The only time Larry's clean
is when he's in the shower.

WORD LIST

clean	gets	knees	seat
clothes	goes	Larry	shower
dirty	hands	Larry's	the
ears	he	matter	time
eyes	he's	neck	toes
face	hour	no	what
feet	in	nose	when
fingers	is	only	where

About the Author

Bobbie Hamsa was born and raised in Nebraska and has a Bachelor of Arts Degree in English Literature. She is an advertising copywriter for Bozell & Jacobs, Inc., writing print, radio, and television copy for many accounts, including "Mutual of Omaha's Wild Kingdom," the five-time Emmy Award winning wild animal series. She is the author of the popular series of books called Far-Fetched Pets, also published by Childrens Press. Bobbie lives in Omaha with her husband, Dick Sullivan, and children, John, Tracy, and Kenton.

About the Artist

Paul Sharp graduated from the Art Institute of Pittsburgh.
He has worked for the Curtis Publishing Company as Art Director of Child Life magazine.
At the present time he works as a free-lance artist at his home in Indianapolis, Indiana.